from the Heights to Enchanted Places

JOHN WILLIAM RICE

Diminuendo Press

To Allen and Brenda or should
it be Brenda and Allen
To memoirs of catching minnows
with straight pen hooks. To
Autumn days trudging through
Woods bereft of leaves after ½ind ga
To long ago memoirs reflected upon
in fondness.
John William Rice

Published by
Diminuendo Press
Imprint of Cyberwizard Productions
1205 N. Saginaw Boulevard #D
PMB 224
Saginaw, Texas 76179

From the Heights to Enchanted Places
Copyright © 2009 Cyberwizard Productions

Individual poems copyright © 2009 John William
Rice

ISBN: 978-1-936021-02-4

First Edition:

DEDICATION

For my sister Rose, may life's passage be gentle on you. Though you are now separated from your soul mate, lifelong friend and partner, do not despair. A new dawn shall break and once more you will be together with your love. Until that time is upon you, enjoy life, enjoy your family because this is the way he would want it to be.

Do not weep sad bitter tears
You had many joy filled years
Though death has separated
You for a little while
Dry your eyes and smile
For he waits beyond the veil
Some day you to will journey on
You will see him standing on the shore
And you will be united forever more

table of contents

FROM THE HEIGHTS

TO

ENCHANTED PLACES

From the Heights to Enchanted Places

Spiraling ever upward
White tipped, feathered wings
Stretching, stretching outwards
Catch every breath of wind
From the distant, sun warmed plain
Circling, circling ever wider
A king of air, of Eyre
Surveys his large domain

Corrupt captains of industry
Sheltered in their ivory towers
Bend their scheming minds
To the business of the day
Maniacal laughter echoes
In white, soundproof rooms
Beady eyes, in pinched, pallid faces
Sparkle, glimmer bright
With the counting of each coin
Scrawny chests puff out
Filled with pompous, sinful pride
As ill gotten gold
Is added to their treasure

My vision changes
Dream thoughts take me
Far from cold reality
To delightful, enchanted places

The moon bright night
Is filled with a wonder
Flickering, dancing, fairy lights

Shimmer upon the meadow green
In breathless anticipation
The captivating, little folk
Wait for their King and Queen

Dryads and sayters
Play their pipes of gold
I lay upon the forest edge
And watch with great delight
A loud "Achoo," escapes my mouth
Suddenly all fairy folk are gone
Fairy lights become fire flies
Disappearing into the light of dawn

A grim Elf Lord
Stands in halls of stone
In the fastness of his keep
Preparing for bitter war

Troubles of all kinds
Pervade the pathways
Of his noble mind
And keep him away
From a restful sleep

I toss and turn
Upon my feather bed
Enchanted visions fade
Quiet thoughts prevail
And I drift way
On a tide of peace
Wrapped up in a golden sail

Darfur, Politics of Genocide

Dust dirt fear,
Women in bright cloth,
Wring their hands,
In despair,
Another night
When savage bodies,
Come in lust,
To thrust themselves,
In to soft
Unprotected flesh,
A young girl screams,
In pain,
From destruction,
Of innocence,
From despair,
Her womanhood,
So brutally, entered,
Then comes,
The thunder
Of roaring guns,
Is it shame
That caused these marauders,
To kill, not only innocence,
But broken, used bodies.
No police, no soldier,
Comes to their aid
Only the bright sun,
Delivers them,
For a brief time,
From the evil of the night,
To soon the dark returns,

3

As does the fear
As does the death,

The Dry Land

The dry land,
Thirstily soaks up,
The few,
Scattered raindrops,
Then lies unquenched,
Barren of life,
Seeds planted,
Die unborn,
Wisps of green grass wither,
White bones bleached,
By the broiling sun,
Cover the landscape,
Piled high,
They rattle loudly
In the searing wind,
Above a vulture circles,
Looking down,
Nothing moves,
On this dry land,
But the shadow of death,

Desire

When two
Are overwhelmed
By desire,
Consumed by loves
Sweet burning fire,
Time it's self
Becomes compressed,
The only sensations left
Are fast beating hearts
And naked flesh
Pressed close
To naked flesh

My First time

In majestic splendor,
Snow capped peaks,
Thrust themselves deep,
In to the blue of summer sky,
Towering, overpowering,
I am overwhelmed,
By my insignificance,
By my mortality,
I turn to see, if others,
My fellow travelers,
Are awake, I wish to share
This awesome moment,
But they have their eyes closed,
Still buried in deep slumber
As I look in awe,
I can only wonder,
Is it like this for others?
When it is their first time?

Children Of The Emerald Isle

They chose Diaspora instead of hunger,
Freedom instead of serfdom,
A strange land over a tyrant's power
They sailed away from beloved homeland,
Proudly bearing their Irish names,
O'Neil, O'Malley, Dougal,
Macauley, Wallace and Keen,
From humble, straw thatched cottages,
In Kerry, Derry and Dublin,
Galway, Limrick and Cork,
To villages in Quebec
To the streets of Muddy York,
They came to till the farmlands,
To plant their roots firm and deep,
They came to escape a famine,
A king's oppressive hand,
Looking for hope and freedom,
In a strange and distant land,
At first they were unwanted,
But they soon won hearts with warm smile,
Now firmly a part of this country,
Are the proud children of the Emerald Isle,

The Short Ones

The pen shall be my sword

The pen shall become my sword,
I will blood it often with ink.
Bringing harm to no just man,
Only wounding the oppressor's pride

A quiet time of rest

Ere life's battle be rejoined,
I need a quiet time to rest,
In some silent valley,
Beside a white doves nest,

Ten thousand drummers

Ten thousand drummers drumming,
Beat a precision rhyme,
Ten hundred thousand soldiers march.
Their feet in perfect time,
A multitude of people watch,
A loud, shouting human flood,
Ten hundred thousand soldiers lie,
Face down in the reddening mud.

In the Midnight of the Morning

In the midnight of the morning
As the sun peeks out of the broken sky
Examine the tendrils of time passing
Through the microscope of your mind

Wander down the pathways
Leading backwards to the dawn
As you listen to words of wisdom
Try to stifle each and every yawn

For the professors and the intellects
Growl angrily into moth eaten beards
As they try to mend Excalibur
With incantations and bitter words

Even if it can be welded back to newness
Who will wield the wholesome blade?
Who has the fortitude to rescue?
The sad, distressed young maid

Will she be forever captive?
To the madness of her dreams
Will her heart be forever fastened?
To her thread bare tortured schemes?
In the midnight of the morning
Inside the madness of your mind
Count backwards from a hundred
Until you come to the end of time

In the midnight of the morning
As the sun peeks out of the broken sky

Examine the tendrils of time passing
Through the microscope of your mind

Waiting

Where are they now
Our kinsmen son?
Why is the air so still?
Will they ever again
Come marching
Over the barren hill
Yonder they went
In the morning,
Full of life, of youth, of pride,
If I were only younger,
I would have been at their side
My bones are too brittle
For marching,
My eyes have grown too dim,
Yet though I stay in our village,
I have sent my soul with them
Hush now, and listen,
What is that I hear?
Wailing away in the distance,
Very low, yet very clear,
Is it our kinsmen
Returning home from war?
Or is it but the bitter wind,
As it blows forever more?

Tomorrow's Dream

Stone cold and gray the newborn day
Children have no place to play.
No parks no fields of green.
No bubbling brook, no fish filled stream.
All that is left is brick and glass.
And dreary, dark, smoke filled sky.
No wonder children just stand and cry.
In their minds do they wonder why?
This is our legacy of greed.
Our all consuming need.
To rape and pillage our mother earth
To take from her anything of worth,
There are no growing trees.
No place for children, to swing up high.
No singing birds fill the morning sky.
No wonder children just stand and cry.
In their minds do they wonder why?
We do not see this as we sleep.
In our graves, so cold and deep,
We do not see the smoke filled sky.
We do not hear our children cry.
But this matters not, for they too shall die.
All that will be left is brick and glass.
And dreary, dark, smoke filled sky.
No wonder the children, just stand and cry.
In their minds do they wonder why?

Burn The Sweet Grass For Me

Burn the sweet grass for me,
Cleanse my body, mind and soul,
Let me soar on high with the eagle,
Run free with the white wolf.
Let the bear become my brother.
Can the pale skin,
Ever walk hand in hand with the red,
In our minds,
Will we ever truly know?
That the earth is indeed,
Our mother
Burn the sweet grass for me,
In the morning light,
So my day and thoughts,
Will become pure
Let my entire being.
Know the wrong that I have done.
Burn the sweet grass for me,
Cleanse my body, mind and soul.
Let me soar on high with the eagle.
Run free with the wild white wolf,
Let the black bear, become my brother.
Can my feet ever walk down
The red man's path,
In my mind,
Will I ever understand?
That this earth,
Is indeed my mother?

Man Child

Euphoria cannot describe
The feelings of joy
That permeates my heart
Mind and soul
Every atom of my being
Is alive with the wonder

In new, pink, wrinkled perfection
My son stretches, yawns
Then suckles contentedly
At his mother's breast

Into this state of ecstasy
Doubtful thoughts intrude
Am I worthy of the task?
Can I guide him down
Life's waiting journey

Such dark thoughts
Must be for tomorrows dawn
For now I will treasure
This moment of perfection
With a humble heart
And a contended mind
In awe I watch
My man child sleep

Forgive Me My Brother

Forgive me my brother,
For spilling your blood on the snow,
Thank you for being brave,
For standing still,
So my arrow would fly true.
Bellies that growl from hunger,
In the lodges of my people,
Will be filled with your sweet flesh
None of your great gift will be wasted.
Your flesh will fill our cooking pots.
Your hide will become new moccasins,
We will wear them proudly,
In the days of the long green grass,
The sinews of your body,
Shall be woven in to shoes
For walking over the deep snow,
The marrow of your bones,
Will put fat on the bodies of my children
May your spirit now walk safely,
In lush green fields, beside quiet streams,
I feel the trembling of your body,
As you're gentle heart becomes still.
Your eyes grow dim,
As life fades forever from you,
Again I thank you for your life,
Forgive me my brother,
For spilling your blood on the snow,

Youth Is Not Wasted On The Young

It is not fair for us to say,
That youth is wasted on the young.
It is only some that are young,
Who waste these precious fleeting days,
To those that in ignorance,
Squander these wonder years,
At their door step,
Cannot be laid total blame
They do but emulate, imitate,
What we ourselves have done.
We must ennoble them,
If they are to take up noble cause,
They must write these truths,
So deep, they will ever be in their mind.
Anger begets anger war begets war,
Peace begets peace and greater than even this,
Love begets love.
They young must forever learn,
To go forth with out stretched hand,
Filled with the olive branch,
Not the sharp, blood stained sword.
Youth is not truly wasted on the young,
It is we, who should know better,
It is we who have wasted it for them.

Silver Birch

Silver birch with green leaves,
Leaves that always dance,
And pirouette in the wind.
We often pass you by,
Never giving you a second glance,
Silver birch, with yellow leaves,
Falling fast in autumn storm,
This raiment of your summer's glory,
Will keep small creatures warm,
Silver birch, without any leaves,
Waiting patiently for the spring
When once more you will wear
Your radiant green crown,
And be a place where birds come to sing.

By Love Possessed

To ourselves at least,
We must be true.
We must admit to each other,
If to no one else,
That we are by love possessed,
There can be no other cause
For our all consuming need,
Our desire for consummating lust,
In all honesty, we can say,
We did not mean to deceive.
To betray another's trust,
To be so enraptured, so captured,
By our bodies, pounding thrust.
When we think within ourselves,
There are no more of loves,
Mysterious uncharted seas,
We suddenly are amazed,
When we discover,
As yet unknown, deeper bliss,
More wondrous ecstasy,
Greater warmth, new found tenderness

It Is Not By Desire

It is not by desire,
That love is sustained.
For desire unchecked,
Consumes all in its path,
In the intensity of its flame,
Yet desire should not be,
Completely put from mind.
For in the scheme of things,
It too has its place.
But real love,
Is born of other things,
And is only found
When one gives the gift,
The gift of self,
In complete surrender,
Then there is no more self,
No more selfish I or me,
But only thoughts of us,
Of giving pleasure,
And brief bright moments,
Filled with touch, caress,
And wondrous splendor,

Blended

Brown and yellow,
Black and white
We are all the same.
In the darkness of the night,
Any difference's then,
Are only in the mind
Would not humanity
Be better off
 If we were born color blind

A Glass Of Wine

A glass of wine,
Lungs now filled,
With the sweet smoke
Of Mary-Jane,
I shed no more tears,
I feel no more pain.
I gently drift,
Among distant stars,
I hold the moon,
Fast in my hands,
And at last,
I more fully understand,
There is no distance,
No beginning,
No fate full end,
We are as one,
We began as one,
There is no mystery,
No sudden dark,
Children play in the park,
They hunger not,
But for today,
They give more,
Than they take,
Their laughter echoes,
Lingers as they go
I still have my glass of wine,
One more puff,
Of sweet Mary-Jane,
I have no more tears,
I feel no more pain.

Heart Of The City

Though you may grow weary,
Of your days with in me,
You may grow tired,
Of my noise, my dirt, my dust,
You may try to run away,
Play in the green fields,
Surrounding me
But it will be only for a day.
You cannot forever escape me,
Like a moth,
That is forever drawn,
By the bright candle flame,
When the wind whispers my name,
You will return to me,
You are youth,
And youth is my builder,
Youth is my corner stone.
Yet even when,
You become old and withered,
And are of no more good,
Your dust will become my dust,
And we will be one forever.

Madness Is As Madness Does

Madness is as madness does,
Can one escape
With enough dream dust?
What is fantasy?
What is real?
Are both just a part,
Of life's spinning wheel,
When we dream,
Are we awake?
Will we ever know
What has substance
Or what is fake?
Madness is as madness does
Can one escape
With enough dream dust?
Do we desire
Or do we lust?
Is death our final goal?
Does reality lie beyond?
At the end,
Of some black hole,
Madness is as madness does,
Can one escape
With enough dream dust?

Listening

I paused,
A while,
To listen,
And watch,
The world go by
Over the noise,
The endless din,
I heard,
A child's cry,
It was a sad,
A lonely weeping
A cry for love,
A crust of bread,
Who shall tell
This homeless waif,
That hope,
That dreams
Are dead?
Too young,
Too innocent,
Too new in world,
To understand,
The cold,
Sad reality,
Of man's,
Inhumanity to man,
I paused,
A while,
To listen,
And watch,
The world pass by

Over its noise,
It's endless din,
I heard,
A child's cry,

The Lonely Bugler

I hear a lonely bugler play
As the day slowly slips away
Another soldier
Some ones son, some ones brother
Has died in this endless war
And as the lonely bugler plays
I wonder
How many more

How many more soldiers
Fathers, sons and brothers
How many boys
Barley old enough to shave
Will leave the comfort
Of their home and family
And forever lie
In some cold and lonely grave

How long before
This call to arms has ended
How long before
The cannons no longer roar
And rockets no longer blaze
Across the summer sky
How long until little children
No longer have to die

How long before we live
In peace and love
For inside were pretty much the same
It shouldn't matter the color of our skin

How many times we pray
Or our given name
We must learn to live as brothers
Or we can all learn how to die
How long before the guns are silent
And rockets no longer blaze
Across the summer sky
How long before babies
No longer have to die

I hear a lonely bugler play
As the day slowly slips away
Another sailor
Some ones son, some ones brother
Has died in this endless war
And as the lonely bugler plays
And the day slips away
I can only wonder
How many more

Let This Day Be With me

The day is with me,
Its wild seasons
Punish me for my doubt,
For my disbelief,
In the goodness,
It can bring,
I am punished,
For the lack of love,
Love of self,
Love of others,
I am punished,
For not grabbing
Every precious moment,
For not holding fast,
To the dreams,
This new day offers.
I let its newness,
Slip away,
As I have,
So often done before
And as the sun fades,
In to another time of dark,
There is only
One question,
That now fills my mind.
Will there ever be,
Another precious day,
For me to squander

As The Twilight Fades

My needs are now less,
As are my desires,
Few embers still glow.
Of my once raging fires,
My eyes have grown dim,
From the passage of time,
I chase fleeting thoughts,
Through the depths of my mind,
Yesterday is much closer,
Than the things of today,
Is that the grim reaper
Coming to take me away?
The blossoms are bright,
The grass much greener this spring,
I will try to hold on,
And see what winter will bring.
Perhaps it will be easier,
For me to let go,
Of life's last fragile thread,
When the land is covered with snow
Please scatter my ashes,
On the waves of the sea,
So little fishes,
Will have a meal out of me

And As Night Falls

And as night falls
In the tenements
In the ghettos
In the streets of desolation
Man, woman, child
Stare out of
Lighted, blighted windows
Into the gathered dark
Seeking for
A sliver of salvation

In the distance
A barking dog
A crying child
A shouting man
A shouting woman
Fill the night air
With their hopelessness

And as night falls
In the parks
In the laneways
In the suburbs
In the streets of resolution
Man, woman, child
Stare out of decorated windows
Into the gathered dark
Filled with absolution

In the distances
A barking dog

A laughing child
A singing man
A singing woman
Fill the night air
With their hopefulness

And as night falls
In the lane ways
In the alleys
In empty lots
In the houses of addiction
Man, woman, child
Stare out of glassless windows
Into the gathered dark
Wrapped tight
In deaths affliction

In the distance
A whining dog
A weeping child
A weeping man
A weeping woman
Fill the night air
With their abandonment
And as night falls
In the tenements
In the ghettos
In the streets of desolation
Man, woman, child
Stare out of
Lighted, blighted windows
Into the gathered dark
Seeking for

A sliver of salvation

Midnight Breaks

The minute hand ticks past
The black numbers
On the white clock face
Midnight breaks
It shatters on the sharp edges
Of the new made day

We wait, anticipating
We wait, wondering
We wait, dreaming

And as the shards of darkness fall
And as a new day is born into fullness
The clock hand still ticks
Past black numbers on white clock faces

Newness comes
Oldness fades
Life and death
Pass and change
And yet
Each ticking moment
Seems to be the same

Many minute hands
Tick past
Many black numbers
On white clock faces
Midnight breaks
It shatters on
The sharp edges

Of the new made day

Unnamed

I hear the wind, feel the wind,
Watch my life' shadows passing,
Bitter tears, lonely days,
Girls of summer gaily laughing,
Empty dreams, raindrops falling,
Wild flying geese are calling,
As the wind and day are dying,
Still the lonely sky is crying.

In The Fastness Of The Forest

In the fastness of the forest,
Under bows of leafy green,
A red man walks in safety,
With his wife and children,
But at night his dreams are bitter,
Filled with men of pale skin,
They ride great beasts,
Their weapons thunder.
They will come, kill and plunder,
In the night a great chief trembles,
Seeing the death, that is now waiting,
In the morning, he will seek out the shaman,
In the morning, he will look for answers.
In his dream, his world changes,
Gone now the deer and forest
Gone the tepees of his people
Gone his way of life forever
In its place, the land is barren,
Empty of all its goodness,
In the night a chieftain wakens,
His heart is heavy, from his dreaming,
In the fastness of the forest,
Under bows of leafy green,
A red man walks in safety,
With his wife and children

The Hounds Of War

Once more, string the bow,
Polish the sword,
Sharpen the lance.
The hounds of war,
Have been unleashed,
Blood will be shed,
Honor will be won.
Glory will be
The order of the day,
Brother will once more
Kill brother.
The green land,
Will again run red,
It will always be this way,
Until we learn,
That we must walk in peace.

The Hunt

The morning was rich,
Pale and deep,
Blue and cold, lying still,
But the blowing horn,
Did rise all from their sleep,
Even the fox upon the hill,
Even the fox upon the hill,

Their tunics were red,
They gleamed in the sun.
Their steeds were all fresh
And ready to run,
And the hounds were ready to kill
The hounds were ready to kill.

There was frost in the meadow,
There was frost on the trees,
The hunter's blood ran warm not cold,
The wily fox too was ready for the game,
So they ran, as the day grew old
They ran, as the day grew old.

But even the swiftest fox grows weary,
And will seek a safe place to rest.
So he looked for a soft place in the ground,
Dig deep into mother earth's breast,
Dig deep into mother earth's breast.

The hunters were not willing,
To give up the day,
Their hounds still wanted the kill.

They rode home filled with a hunter's pride,
Carrying the bloody fox from the hill,
Carrying the bloody fox from the hill

A Star's Demise

In bright flaming fury,
You blaze across the darkness.
Fire fills the sky with your passing.
Trees bow in the wind you make.
In fear, wild creatures quake
You shake the earth,
The quiet sea turns into steam.
Did you come from the Pleiades?
Was Orion's Belt your home?
What made you give up your glory?
Seek out self-destruction.
You have no more splendor
There is nothing now left,
But a memory of your greatness

Interlude

I take this time for reflection,
To consider my thoughts and words,
Do I need to explain them?
Will those who read them understand?
Will they glance at them only briefly?
Or will they take the time to study?
Do they find themselves enlightened?
Are they amused or are they frightened?
By the rantings and the ravings,
By the tortured tangled twistings of my mind.
As I bare my soul before you,
I hope that I don't bore you.
At least not until you pass half way.
There is one thing I need mention,
Before your journey does continue,
I do not have the intention,
To take a critic's words to heart,
Perhaps a few of my verses will inspire,
Light some noble cleansing fire,
That will brighten a dark and lonely mind.
You now may continue,
Down the path I've set before you
And leave your doubts
And troubled past behind

Reflections

At night as I walk,
Through the shadows,
That lie on the streets
Empty and still,
I think of my past,
When I was a clown,
And traveled,
With those of my kind,
I was so proud,
To be in the center ring
Surrounded by my friends,
I was over whelmed,
By the smell of the grease paint,
The roar of the crowd,
When the performance was over,
There was stillness,
A closeness shared
A happiness with in
Now there is only sadness,
The magic has ended,
My past is reflected,
In the glint of muddy waters,
Lying in pools,
After the rain,

A Time When Giants Walked

Their names will echo proudly,
Down through the halls of time,
Seared for ever in human heart and mind,
They had clay feet, like other mortals,
Yet towered high above the crowd,
They ennobled all who would listen,
To there impassioned words,

"We will fight them on the beaches,
In towns, cities on village green,
We will never surrender,"
Churchill spoke these words,
Full of courage and of power,
Guiding England through her darkest days,
It was also her finest hour,

A little, thin brown man,
No one would look at twice,
A quiet self-effacing hero,
Challenged an empires might,
He used no sword, no bullets, no bomb,
It was with words of peace,
That he won his fight,

"I have a dream," spoke a noble man,
A great dream, for all to share,
A dream of hope, of peace of love,
With courage he courted death,
Putting others above himself,
Giving up his life because he cared,

In prison his life was molded,
By things no man should endure,
Doubt and dross were burnt away,
Leaving a heart and spirit pure,
With kindness, he broke his people's chains,
Ended apartheid's terrible curse,
He bore no grudge against his jailers,
But turned the other cheek,
With great love and courage,
He is a bright beacon for the meek,

It is now time to read the honor roll,
Sound trumpets as the names are read,
Churchill, Gandhi, King, Mandela,
Only one now remains of these mighty men,
Only one of these giants left to treasure,
He showered love upon us all,
We must return it in good measure,
We truly are among the blessed,
To have lived in these days,
In a time when giants walked.

African Princess

A dark ebony beauty waits, partly hidden,
In shadows and leafy green,
Filtered, dancing sunbeams,
Reveal elegant delicate features,
A gentle heart beats wildly from fear,
Beneath soft perfect breasts,
A civilized mind does not understand,
Cannot in its depths comprehend?
This terrible thing that is taking place,
Tall, savage, blonde haired, bearded men,
Men of milk white skin,
Strip her of clothes, decency, dignity,
Brutally, ravish her repeatedly,
Heavy steel chains, gouge deep,
Blood oozes from soft dark skin,
Taken suddenly from sunlight,
Thrust into foul smelling darkness,
A mind retreats from reality,
Not knowing how such a thing can be,
After all she is the daughter of a king

Four Horsemen

High above me, in a cloud filled sky,
Lit dimly by the veiled moon,
Four horsemen gather on death head steeds,
Their faces wear the mask of doom,
Lightning flashes from stone cold eyes,
Thunder echo's loudly as they ride.

I tremble when I see them,
Though they have passed my way before,
Their names are burned deep with in my soul,
They are greed, pestilence, death and war,
They bring with them the apocalypse,
Their swords drip red with blood.

They laugh, when they see me cower,
Then with out paying further heed,
They drive sharp steel spurs in to bony flanks,
In voices that would cause the dead to quake,
Call loudly to their steeds.

I tremble with fear as I watch them,
Ride through stormy skies once more,
In dread, unable to breathe, I wonder,
What lands do they intend to plunder,
These horsemen of the apocalypse,
Greed, pestilence, death and war
It is we who in our pride have called them,
To ride through our lands once more,
We prefer the sword to the olive branch,
So now the deadly horsemen once more ride,
Greed, pestilence, death and war,

Belly Of My Mind

I am in deep,
Far past,
The belly,
Of my mind,
My thoughts,
Are a quagmire
Twisting, turning
Taking me,
To unpleasant places,
Places best forgot,
Best not returned to,
But like,
An unbridled,
Wild horse,
They run free.
Not caring,
About the pain,
Not caring,
That I relive,
Unwanted memories,
Dredged from,
Some deep place,
Far past,
The belly,
Of my mind.

And Now To Sleep

And now to sleep,
Perchance to dream,
Of a time that's gone away,
And can never be again.

Jerusalem

Jerusalem, city of David,
Holy city of God,
Wounded heart of Israel,
Symbol of hope,
Symbol of peace
You inspire the faithful,
Yet are filled with despair,
War drums echo,
In cobbled streets,
We pray for peace,
But the blood runs deep,
Blood of martyrs,
Blood of the saints,
Blood of the innocent,
Even the blood of Christ,
Has stained your dust
From Temple Mount,
To the place of the skull,
The sinner's crawl,
Seeking forgiveness,
Seeking redemption,
Seeking salvation,
We wail at the Wailing Wall,
Do our prayers,
Fall on unhearing ears.
The quiet of the night,
Is shattered by the blast,
Of another bomb,
Dust slowly settles,
A child cries in pain,
More blood,

Blood of innocent
Blood of martyr,
Join together,
Seep through the cracks,
Between worn cobble stones,
Oh Jerusalem,
Holy city of God,
We pray for your peace,

My Mate

I desire not the shrinking violet,
Or the delicate flower,
I desire a woman of the hour,
One proud of her feminine power,
One of true intellect,
But not of the same mind,
One who will not be blind?
To my faults or my mistakes,
A listener who will listen deep,
More than just a body,
That keeps me warm when I sleep,
A partner that will stand true,
Through the passages of time,
Two sides of the same coin,
Bonded fast as one

A Rapper Times Two

In the ghetto, a rapper raps,
Words of despair,
Does any one care
For the child,
Running wild?
Gangbanger, getting busted
Never should have trusted,
A gun that was rusted.
Bo peep, black sheep,
A woman weeps,
For her man,
Can't understand,
Death and destruction,
Tear the walls down.
Make way for new construction,
Child dies, in a drive by.
Mother's weep, can't sleep,
Empty bed, her baby's dead.
Gangbanger fled,
Gets busted,
Never should have trusted
A gun that was rusted,
In a jewelry store,
A wrapper wraps,
Ties dainty bow,
On hidden treasure,
A young man's hopes,
And dreams inside,
His mind is filled,
With pictures,
Of his blushing bride,

In streets dirty and worn,
Alone, forlorn,
A rapper raps.

Hung Over

I awake, my eyes blood shot, bleary,
My bones ache, I am so weary,
Was it too many beers?
No, this pain could not come,
From a thing,
That brings so much delight,
It must have been,
The late hour of the night,
That causes my head to pound,
And painfully throb,
I pull on day old socks,
Sweaty beer stained shirt,
Getting ready for another day,
Getting ready for the job,
Stomach, queasy, churning,
From the smell of frying eggs,
I walk to the coffee pot,
On weak, wobbly legs,
The scalding hot caffeine fix,
Kicks my body into over drive,
I realize that I am still alive,
A cracked, dirty mirror,
Reflects eyes, bloodshot, bleary,
My bones ach,
Because I am still weary.

Poet And Soldier

Can this duality of my nature,
Some how in harmony be joined,
In the daylight, in the scorching desert,
I take the lives of my enemy,
Both my hands, my very soul,
Are stained, deep dark red, from their blood,
Children, women, bring destruction,
Wrapped tightly around their bodies,
I do not understand this quest for Holiness,
I cannot make sense of this futility,
I was born to far gentler things,
When night descends, I seek my kinder half,
I use my right hand, my blood stained hand,
To write words of peace, words of love,
But most times these words are lost,
Some where in the depths of depravity,
In the mind of this killing machine,
I long to see my new born son,
To hold my woman, close in the dark night,
Will the dogs of war ever be leashed?
I have but one hope, one repeated prayer,
That when my son makes his rite of passage,
The need for soldiers will be long past,
And a poet's words will be honored.

Let A Little Child Lead You

When the world is too much with you,
And your heart is filled with pain,
When you have fallen down so many times,
You doubt if you can rise again,
Let a little child lead you,
Take an outstretched hand,
Though they are of tender years,
Some how the seem to understand,
"Please don't cry," they whisper,
As they hug you tight,
Have pleasant dreams when you sleep,
Tomorrow things will be all right,

They give their love so freely,
Ask for so little in return,
The lessons they can teach us,
Are ones that we should learn,
There is no happiness like a child's laughter,
No sadness like a child's tears.

When you are lost and lonely,
And have no place to turn,
Look deep with in your self,
Remember the lessons you have learned,

Let a little child lead you,
Take their outstretched hand,
Though they are of tender years,
Some how the seem to understand,
They whisper as they hug you tight,
Have sweet dreams when you sleep,

Tomorrow things will be all right.

Little Black Bellies

Little black bellies,
Distended from starvation,
Limbs pipe stem thin,
Bones so brittle,
A gentle wind,
Could break them,
Mothers weep,
Tears of dust,
At least the ones,
The few, who still have,
The strength to weep,
Flies nest,
Lay eggs,
In oozing wounds,
I change channels,
Before taking another bite,
Of my burger,
Take a sip,
Of cold foamy beer,
For me it is,
Far too cruel,
A thing to watch,
To listen too,
If I hurry,
I can make the happy hour,
Do your homework kids,
Before I return,
There is ice cream,
For desert,
Little black bellies,
Distended from starvation,

Limbs pipe stem thin,
Bones so brittle,
A gentle wind,
Could break them

Faith

From crypt, from tomb,
The stone rolled way,
Open now place of the dead,
From with in the body gone,
Who did this deed of sacrilege?
Women come to pray and weep,
The watchman lies fast asleep.
A promise made is remembered,
Has this promise now been kept?
Yet even the disciples doubt,
That such a thing could ever be.
But feet once walked across a sea.
People bound by sin were free,
The dead were called to live again,
Gone were bitter tears and pain,
The sick were raised from their bed,
The blood of an innocent lamb was shed,
A king wore a crown of thorns.
If this is a gift you desire to receive,
Then in your heart you must believe.

A Grand Canal

Gather the waters,
That lie in the mountains
Dam up the brook,
The swift bubbling stream,
Let all of this water,
Flow ever eastward,
To become the great Canadian dream,
They came from the valleys,
They came from the mountains,
They came from the forests,
They came from the sea,
The land that they loved,
Was becoming a desert,
No matter the cost,
They could not let this be.
They would dig a great ditch,
Across the wide prairie,
It would carry,
The life giving water,
From the shining mountains,
All the way to the sea,
Gather all the water,
That lie in the mountains,
Dam up the brook,
The swift bubbling stream,
Let all of this water,
Flow ever eastward,
To become our Canadian dream,

Girls Of Summer

Bikini bottomed, barely covered,
Soft warm flesh,
Waiting to be discovered,
Seductive oiled bodies glisten,
Browning in the summer sun,
Light thoughts dance,
Through girlish minds,
Laughter chimes as men glance,
Bold stares returned by impish grin,
Eyes and thoughts then wander,
Idly to other things,
Forgotten for now, work, school,
In low voices, are secrets shared,
Of new loves, of those old and lost,
Of hearts broken, of hearts mended,
They games they play before surrender
This is how they spend each day,
The bikini bottomed girls of summer.

In Kerouac's Footsteps

Four tread bare tires,
Nearly worn to the rim,
Churn up swirls of dust,
As we drive down,
An empty desolate road,
That winds its way,
Through stunted,
Shriveled cornfields,
No scarecrow needed here,
The oppressive heat,
Is a constant reminder
Of New York summers,
Melted, oozing tarmac,
Sticking to bottoms of feet,
That protrudes through,
Broken heeled, hole filled shoes,
The only relief,
From copper colored sky,
A broken fire hydrant,
Even the old, play like children,
In the refreshing coolness,
I find guilty pleasure,
In sweaty couplings,
In dark dank, fetid ally's,
The bright sun,
Brings shame, not forgiveness,
Stray, mangy dogs bark,
As we roll down dust filled streets,
Of small, bald headed prairie towns,
A light flickers on briefly,
Then flickers off again,

I can only wonder,
If a frustrated townie,
Looking at a future, filled with nothing,
Will find a little pleasure,
In sweaty couplings,
Under sweat stained covers,
My thoughts my existence,
I write down,
On a roll of barely used,
Toilet paper, stolen,
From a one pump gas station,
On the corner, of a dust filled street,
In another nameless,
Bald headed prairie town.

Precious Stone

A precious stone in brilliance glitters,
Clasped tight in filigreed gold,
Proudly displayed on white delicate finger,
Symbol of promised love, symbol of fidelity,
Symbol of death, symbol of destruction,
Symbol of innocence lost, of innocence taken,
In the dark, a hundred guns thunder,
More young bodies are needed,
More slaves are required,
They must dig deep for precious stones.
A sparkling gem for a gun, a fair exchange,
A warlord takes his pleasure,
Then in disgust kills the conquered,
In a village, women weep in anguish,
They have lost all their children,
Bodies are needed for cannon fodder,
In the dark, a young girl cries in fear and hunger,
When day breaks she will dig for treasure
Precious stones in brilliance glitter,
Clasped tight in filigreed gold,
Proudly displayed on white delicate fingers,

The Way Things Should Be

A woodcutter cuts his wood,
A farmer farms his land,
A fisherman brings,
His catch from the deep,
Things are as they were planned,
A mother suckles
A baby at her breast,
Deep in the forest,
Songbirds build their nest,
Lovers snuggle, bill and coo,
As they were meant to do,
Frogs catch flies,
In fresh water ponds,
Fire flies flicker in the night,
Cows and horses,
Take their rest,
Waiting for the morning light,
Newborn lambs,
Frolic in the meadow green,
Cuddly kittens,
Play with a ball of string,
Stop, breath deep,
The fresh country air,
Life indeed,
Can be a good thing

Nickel

In the belly of the earth,
The cold shiny metal waits,
Men, mole like, burrow deep,
Men, ant like, scurry busily,
About there appointed task,
There is no day or night,
In this hot, dusty, rocky tomb
The roof groans, creaks above them,
"Fire in the hole," echoes in the darkness,
The earth shakes and trembles,
Not willing to give up its treasure,
The cost is high, when men go deep,
In sweat, in blood, in broken bones,
In bodies mangled, in lives ended,
After each death, the bustle continues,
The shiny metal is quickly swallowed,
More, more, more, the greedy cry,
Machines of war roll off the assembly line.
In the belly of the earth,
The cold shiny metal waits.

Softness Of The Summer

In the softness of the summer,
As I lie upon white sand,
I look in awe and wonder,
At the beauty of the sky.
I long to be on board
The cloud ships sailing by.
Who is their captain?
How many in the crew?
What distant lands of mystery,
Are they sailing to?
I let my mind go with them,
As heaven's cannons roar,
Lighting flashes form their guns,
This is a mighty war.
I am brought back to reality,
By warm drops of summer's rain.
In haste I leave the sandy beach,
Knowing I will return again.

Bulawayo

Dust devils dance
In the streets of Bulawayo

Markets and granaries
Once full of harvests plenty
Stare starkly in their emptiness
This bread basket of Africa
Has become a ghetto
Filled with the hungry

Heavily booted, storm trooper feet
Echo loudly on cobbled streets
No one has come this day
To cast a vote for freedom

Dust devils dance
In the streets of Bulawayo
As the sun descends
As another night of fear begins

We, who live in a privileged state,
Should in righteous indignation
Condemn the tyrant,
That in corruptive power
Tramples on the few shards
Now left, of his people's dignity
Lest we in our silence
We who do not care to speak
Are in our final days
Condemned by a higher Judge

Dust devils dance in the
Streets of Bulawayo

A child, rail thin
Coughs then weeps
One last death rattle
Is swallowed by the night wind
A smiley faced despot
Contentedly sleeps
His belly full of food
Stolen from a child's mouth
A child that once laughed
And joyfully played
In the streets of Bulawayo

I Dream Of Whales

I dream of whales.
Their music fills my mind.
I dive into the depths,
And swim with all my passion.

I am at last
Unfettered by the land.
I float in ecstasy,
Among the pod,
That has claimed me
As their own

I dream of whales.
In the night,
Their shapes and music
Delight me.
In my sleeping hours,
The power of my vision
Transports me to
A mystic, mysterious realm

I dream of whales.
I dance to the
Music of their song
When day has broken
And I am gone,
Will the whale's dream of me

Song Of The Winds

Willows growing by the water
Listen to songs of the east wind
And to its enchanting laughter
East wind sings stories of the sea
Of seals that frolic in the foam
Of coral seas and mighty waves
That thunder on the shore
Willows weep when east wind leaves
Begging it for more

Willows growing by the water
Listen to songs of the south wind
And to its captivating laughter
South wind sings of distant lands
Where dusky maidens dance
With red flowers in their hair
Willows weep when south wind leaves
And wish that they were there

Willows growing by the water
Listen to songs of the west wind
And to its charming laughter
West wind sings of mountain spires
Where rivers are new born
Of golden eagles soaring high
Willows weep when south wind leaves
Wishing they could fly

Willows growing by the water
Listen to songs of the north wind
And to its enthralling laughter

North wind sings of polar bears
Of frozen icy lands
Where homes are made of snow
Willows weep when north wind leaves
Wishing they could go

Tired willows nod their heads
And in wonder gaze
As moonbeams and fairy lights
Shimmer upon the waves.

Kings, Nobles, Common Men

Kings, nobles, common men,
All come to the same bitter end,
Our mortality we cannot transcend,
Our fate we cannot escape,
Since the moment we were conceived,
Our dark final hour lay in wait,
Will our soul then be free?
Flee to a better place,
Wander safe in pastures green,
For ever in a state of grace,
Or will we lie in our tomb,
In earth's dark, damp, moldy womb,
Nothing more than food for worms,
Until at last comes the day,
When we return to our beginning clay,
Kings, nobles, common men,
All come to the same bitter end,

From The Valley To The Mountains

The raging river wends its way
Confined, constrained, guided
Between snow capped spires
My thoughts wind their way
Confined, constrained, guided
By narrowness and bigotry
By the will of others
I dare not let them escape
Lest they encourage and inspire
Priests, pastors, rabbis
People of likeminded will
Place barriers before me
Insurmountable heights I must scale
The raging river wends its way
Confined, constrained, guided
It roars through rocky gorges
And at last breaks free
My thoughts wind their way
Confined, constrained, guided
Yet they too have their escape
Journey far beyond the pale
I take the river's journey
From the valley to the mountains

Bleeding, raw, my gnarled hands
Claw at craggy outcroppings
Upwards ever upwards
To where peaks of snowy beauty
Call me to be more
To be better than myself
I look backwards, downwards

To where in silence
The valley in its greenness rests
For a long moment
My tired eyes linger
On the place of my beginning
My gaze returns to the mountains
To the way set before me
To the new day that beckons
From the valley to the mountains
From the darkness to the dawn
Bleeding, raw, my gnarled hands
Pull me upwards, pull me on

BIOGRAPHY

John William Rice was born November 30, 1942 in Iroquois Falls Ontario - the fifth child in a family of six. Shortly after the war, the family moved to a small farm in Sharp Township and when John was five they moved again, this time to a small farm near the village of Charlton Ontario.

He left school when he was 15 and, after working at many jobs in the cities of Toronto and Vancouver (as well as other places) he went back to school through a government sponsored program. After completing high school, he studied electronics at Northern College of Applied Arts and Technology.

He was hired in 1971 by International Nickel Company as an instrument technician and retired in 2005 after 34 years. His wife died in 2003 from cancer, and both sons, Matthew and Andy, are grown so he began looking for a second career.

John had always been an avid reader, so in the winter of 2007 he decided to start writing. After completing a few plays and several short stories, he plunged head first into both a novel and also his first book of poems, *From the Heights to the Enchanted Places*. A second book of poems is planned, as well as several more novels.

John resides in Sudbury Ontario.

Printed in the United States
145263LV00001B/5/P